Discover
THOMAS
JEFFERSON

ARCHITECT • STATESMAN • PRESIDENT

WRITTEN BY PATRICIA A. PINGRY

ILLUSTRATED BY MEREDITH JOHNSON

ideals children's books™

Nashville, Tennessee

Thomas Jefferson was born April 13, 1743, in Shadwell, Virginia.

Thomas loved to read. He read every book in his father's library.

Thomas had six sisters
and one brother.

After his father died,
Thomas helped his mother
with the younger children.

Thomas liked to go on
long walks with his oldest
sister Jane. They collected
leaves and insects and rocks.

He took them home to study.

Sometimes Thomas
played his violin while
Jane sang.

Thomas was a good student.
He studied fifteen hours
every day. Then he played
his violin for three more hours.

Thomas grew to be six
feet two inches tall. He
wore his long red hair
tied back in a ponytail.

Thomas studied the law.
He wanted to learn
everything he could.

Virginia was one of thirteen colonies owned by England. The colonies had to pay a lot of money in taxes. Many men did not like to pay these taxes.

Sometimes they had to sell their land
to pay England. Thomas spoke out
against these taxes. But he knew war
over the taxes would come.

After talk of war, Thomas went home. He planned to build his house on top of a mountain. He called the mountain Monticello,

which means "little mountain" in
Italian. Thomas planted fruit
trees on the mountain. And he
began to build a brick house.

One day Thomas met a
young widow named
Martha Wayles Skelton.

They liked to play music
together. She played the piano.
Thomas played his violin.

Thomas and Martha
were married and
moved into Monticello.

They had two daughters.

Thomas built a bigger house.
He planted more gardens.

He bought more books.
Thomas was very happy.

In 1776, Thomas was asked
to write the Declaration of
Independence.

He wrote, "All men are
created equal."

On July 4, 1776, Congress
passed the Declaration of
Independence.

People cheered when it was
read. But England did not cheer.
War began for independence.

After the war, America
was a free country.

Thomas became
secretary of state for
the new country.

In 1796, Thomas was elected vice-president.

And in 1800, Thomas was elected the third president of the United States.

In 1803, Thomas bought a large area of land called the Louisiana Purchase.

He sent a Corps of Discovery led by Meriwether Lewis to explore this land.

They brought back maps,
plants, and animals that
Thomas had never seen.

After eight years as
president, Thomas was
tired. He wanted to go
back home to Monticello.

23

Now Thomas walked
through the woods as
he had as a child.

He held races for
his grandchildren.

He rebuilt Monticello.
And he kept inventing.

He invented a bookstand so
he could read five books at
one time. And he bought
more and more books.

People came from all
over the world to visit
with Thomas.

Sometimes fifty people stayed
all night. Sometimes Thomas
didn't know who they all were.

In 1814, the British army burned the library in Washington, D.C. Thomas sold his 7,000 books to the government.

His books started the Library
of Congress. Thomas said, "I
cannot live without books."
So he bought more books.

Thomas wanted to start
a new school.

He drew up plans for
the buildings. He chose
the books for the library.

He helped select teachers.

Thomas watched as his
school was built. It became
the University of Virginia.

Thomas was president, statesman, and architect. His picture is on the two-dollar bill and on the nickel. We built a monument to remember him.

But most of all, we remember his words, "All men are created equal."